The Unfurling of Silent Wings

In the quiet depths of night,
Whispers dance on gentle air,
Shadows stretch in silver light,
Dreams arise without a care.

Feathered hopes begin to glide,
Through the realms of softest breeze,
A silent song that dreams confide,
Carried forth with tranquil ease.

Each heartbeat speaks of freedom,
Every sigh, a wish unspooled,
In the stillness, there's a kingdom,
Where the heartache's softly fueled.

Wings unfurl in moonlit grace,
A tapestry of hidden flight,
From the darkness, find my place,
In the soft embrace of night.

Now I soar beyond the pain,
Leaving echoes far behind,
With each lift, I break the chain,
In the freedom that I find.

Chronicles of an Unaccompanied Soul

In the mirror of the stars,
I find solace in the void,
Journeys etched in silver scars,
Paths unknown, yet unexplored.

Amidst the thrumming city lights,
Loneliness wraps like a shroud,
Yet in the shadows, hope ignites,
Whispers call me, soft but loud.

With each step, I gather tales,
Of moments lost and dreams regained,
Through the storms and quiet gales,
Life's tapestry is intertwined.

Wanderer, seeking the unseen,
In valleys deep, on mountain high,
Through every heartbeat, I've been keen,
Searching truth beneath the sky.

In solitude, my spirit thrives,
With every breath, I carve my role,
As the world around me strives,
I embrace the unfurling soul.

The Hush Between Heartbeats

In the quiet of the night,
Soft whispers take their flight.
Moments linger, truth unfolds,
In the silence, life beholds.

Shadows dance against the walls,
Echoes of the heart's soft calls.
Each breath held, a secret shared,
In the stillness, we are bared.

Time suspends, the world slows down,
In this peace, we lose the frown.
Every heartbeat, a gentle sigh,
In love's hush, we learn to fly.

Stars above, a guiding light,
Shimmer softly, cold and bright.
Each twinkle holds a dream, a wish,
In this moment, life is rich.

So let the silence wrap so tight,
In the hush, find pure delight.
Between the beats, we are free,
In every pause, eternity.

The Wanderer's Reflection

Footsteps echo on the road,
Each turn whispers stories owed.
Mountains high, valleys low,
In the journey, wisdom grows.

The sun sets, colors blend,
Life's a book with no clear end.
In the wander, truth is found,
In each silence, a heartbeat sound.

Worn-out shoes, a noble tale,
Every gust, a soothing gale.
Clouds drift by, like thoughts unchained,
In the vastness, dreams remain.

Reflections dance in still waters,
Voices of forgotten daughters.
Every face tells of the past,
In the mirror, shadows cast.

So I walk, and I learn more,
Each step opens another door.
With every pause, the lessons weigh,
In wanderlust, I find my way.

Musings at Twilight

As the day slips into night,
Stars awaken, pure and bright.
In twilight's glow, thoughts align,
In the stillness, peace is mine.

Colors blend, a fading hue,
Whispers of the day, anew.
The sky blushes, clouds drift low,
In the moment, hearts will glow.

Crickets sing their evening song,
Nature's choir, sweet and strong.
Moonlight kisses the earth's embrace,
In this magic, I find grace.

Thoughts of love, both lost and found,
In this twilight, I hear the sound.
Moments merge, like shadows play,
In the quiet, I wish to stay.

So let the dusk wrap me tight,
In its arms, find pure delight.
With every sigh, dreams take flight,
In the musings of the night.

The Solitary Bird's Flight

High above on wings of grace,
A solitary bird finds space.
In the blue, it soars and glides,
In the freedom, stillness hides.

With every flap, the world below,
A tapestry of ebb and flow.
Clouds reflect the sun's warm glow,
In the journey, seeds we sow.

Embracing winds, a gentle push,
In solitude, it's never hush.
Chasing horizons, distant dreams,
In every heartbeat, freedom beams.

Time moves slow, the sky unfolds,
Tales of courage, yet untold.
In the heights, where few have gone,
Every breath sings a new dawn.

So let it fly, this bird so brave,
In the sky, it feels the wave.
In solitude, a heart ignites,
In its flight, an endless light.

The Unseen Companion

In shadows, quietly, you abide,
A presence felt, yet not shown wide.
In whispered thoughts, you softly dwell,
A comforting calm, like a distant bell.

Through valleys deep and mountains high,
You walk with me, though none can cry.
In laughter shared and silent sighs,
In every dream, your essence lies.

When night descends, and fears arise,
You cradle hope, beneath the skies.
With gentle nudges, you steer my way,
Through troubled tides and bright bouquet.

In solitude, you hold my hand,
A bond unseen, yet always planned.
In every tear, a smile you cast,
In moments fleeting, you hold steadfast.

Forever close, yet far away,
In every word I fail to say.
You taught me strength, the art of trust,
In every moment, you are a must.

Emptiness in Dawn's Light

A hollow hush before the dawn,
As shadows blend, the light is drawn.
In quiet corners, echoes fade,
Where dreams dissolve, and hopes are laid.

The tepid air, it holds a sigh,
Unraveled thoughts in hues that lie.
A canvas bare, yet full of grace,
Each gentle brush, a soft embrace.

With golden rays, the day takes flight,
Inviting warmth to chase the night.
Yet still within, a void does roam,
A yearning heart that feels like home.

In fleeting beams, I sense the void,
A space of peace, yet still destroyed.
The whispering winds, a ghostly tune,
Under the watch of a waning moon.

In emptiness, I find my peace,
As daylight breaks, my worries cease.
With every dawn, a chance to grow,
In morning light, my spirit flows.

Serene Travels of One

Upon the path where silence breathes,
A traveler wanders, with heart that weaves.
Through fragrant fields, beneath the skies,
In stillness found, where beauty lies.

Each footstep soft, on earth so bare,
With every glance, a secret shared.
A journey taken, yet alone,
In simple sights, the heart has grown.

Through landscapes rich, and sunsets bold,
In whispers soft, past tales unfold.
The winding road, a friend so true,
With every turn, seeks something new.

In forests deep, the echoes play,
The songs of old guide me each day.
With branches swaying, spirits guide,
In nature's arms, I find my pride.

My heart a compass, wild and free,
In quiet moments, I cease to flee.
With open mind and open soul,
The serene travels make me whole.

The Art of Being Alone

In stillness found, the world retreats,
Where solitude and silence meet.
With every breath, a calming hush,
In gentle waves, my worries crush.

A canvas blank, my thoughts take flight,
In colors bright, I paint the night.
With brush in hand, I shape my scene,
The art of self, so rich and keen.

Through whispered winds, I learn to hear,
The subtle voice that draws me near.
In every pause, a chance to grow,
In solitude, my spirit flows.

With each moment, the echoes hum,
In quiet realms, my heartbeats drum.
I dance with shadows, embrace the light,
In every yearning, I find my sight.

The art of being, ever still,
To search within, to bend my will.
In company rare, I learn to thrive,
In solitary grace, I feel alive.

A Solitary Sail on Infinite Seas

In the stillness, waves whisper,
Beneath a canvas of stars bright.
A lone ship drifts on dark waters,
Guided by the moon's soft light.

Gulls cry out in the distance,
Echoes lost to the vast blue.
The horizon calls with persistence,
Chasing dreams the heart once knew.

Salt-kissed air fills my lungs,
Every breath a tale of old.
The sea hums songs yet unsung,
While mysteries begin to unfold.

With each wave, I navigate,
Carving paths through endless night.
Time and tide, they cooperate,
Each moment a fleeting delight.

Embracing solitude's embrace,
This journey fuels the quiet mind.
On infinite seas, I find my place,
In the depth, my soul unwinds.

So I sail with steadfast heart,
Trusting the winds of fate's decree.
From dawn to dusk, I shall not part,
For here, I'm truly free.

The Poetry of Abandonment

In shadows deep, I wander lost,
Echoes haunt the empty halls.
A memoir etched at great cost,
Silence lingers, shadowed calls.

Once vibrant words now fade to grey,
Pages yellowed with time's embrace.
Fragments of a brighter day,
Scattered dreams in a broken place.

I tread lightly on this ground,
Each footfall whispers of the past.
Promises made, now unbound,
Ghosts of love that could not last.

Windows cracked, and doors ajar,
Memories dance in dust and light.
In the distance, a fading star,
Guiding me through the endless night.

Each sigh a verse, each tear a rhyme,
In the poetry of what was lost.
A heart remains trapped in time,
Finding solace despite the cost.

In the Embrace of Quiet Corners

In tucked-away alcoves of thought,
Whispers linger in gentle tones.
Amidst the clutter, solace sought,
A refuge built from silent stones.

Books stacked high in hues of dusk,
Pages yearning to be turned.
Here, the heart sheds daily husk,
And quiet dreams are gently burned.

Light filters softly through the day,
Casting shadows that gently play.
In quiet corners, thoughts mislay,
They drift like clouds, then slip away.

A chair once rocked by love's embrace,
Now holds the weight of all I've known.
Here, memories find their space,
And secrets weave, yet remain alone.

The world outside spins fast and loud,
Yet here, a stillness I have found.
Within these walls, I feel so proud,
In quiet corners, I'm unbound.

Uncharted Waters of the Mind

In the depths where thoughts collide,
Uncharted waters shift and sway.
A map drawn not by fear or pride,
But by the dreams that dance in play.

Currents pull in vibrant hues,
Ideas swirl like leaves in air.
Each tide reveals forgotten clues,
Unveiling realms both rich and rare.

Waves of doubt crash on the shore,
Yet bravery births the unknown.
In this expanse, I long for more,
Each thought a seed that is sown.

Navigating through the mist,
With heart as compass, guiding still.
In these depths, I can't resist,
The call of wisdom, wild and will.

So I dive into the abyss,
With open arms to seize the day.
In uncharted waters, pure bliss,
I chart my course, come what may.

Steps on Dusty Paths

Each step I take on paths of dust,
Leaves behind the dreams I trust.
Whispers of the breeze so sweet,
Guide my weary, wandering feet.

The sun dips low, the shadows grow,
Carving stories in the glow.
With every grain beneath my shoe,
A tale unfolds, both old and new.

Worn out soles and aching bones,
Mark the way to heart's true homes.
Footprints trace where hope has been,
In silence, let the journey begin.

Echoes linger in the night,
Stars above, a guiding light.
Through the dust, the paths will wend,
A journey's start, a journey's end.

The Unknown Within

In quiet corners of the mind,
Secrets of the soul unwind.
Whispers soft, a hidden call,
Echoes in the quiet hall.

Veils of thought, through shadows creep,
Dreams lie waiting, buried deep.
What is lost, what remains bright,
In the depth of endless night?

Through tangled webs of doubts and fears,
The heart reveals its quiet tears.
In solitude, a mirror stands,
Reflecting truths we seldom understand.

Yet within the unknown's embrace,
Lies a strength, a hidden grace.
Journey deep into the core,
To find the self, forevermore.

A Solitary Canvas

On a canvas stretched so wide,
Colors blend, and dreams abide.
Each stroke whispers tales of yore,
Of a heart that seeks for more.

Alone in the stillness of creation,
Imagination fuels elation.
With brush in hand, I paint my plight,
In hues of day and shades of night.

The splatters hide a deep despair,
Yet beauty lingers in the air.
Every line reveals a thought,
In silence, battles bravely fought.

As the layers build, I find my peace,
A solitary dance that will not cease.
In the art, my spirit plays,
A canvas shaped by passing days.

The Voiceless Journey

With each step taken in the dark,
A journey starts, igniting a spark.
Voiceless cries within the soul,
Guide me gently towards my goal.

Unspoken words, a heavy weight,
Beneath the stars, I contemplate.
Paths unworn beneath my tread,
In shadowed dreams, the truth is spread.

Through silent woods and whispering pines,
Nature's chorus softly binds.
With every breath, I'm drawn anew,
The voiceless journey sees me through.

In stillness, I embrace the night,
Find my strength in absence of light.
Each moment held, a sacred thread,
Weaving tales of what was said.

Navigating Through Quiet Waters

Softly gliding, river dreams,
Gentle waves, as daylight gleams.
Whispers float on breezes fair,
Guiding souls through tranquil air.

Stars reflect on liquid glass,
Time slows down as moments pass.
Nature hums a soothing tune,
In the quiet of the noon.

Rustling leaves play with the breeze,
Swaying gently, bending trees.
Every ripple tells a tale,
Of quiet strength, a whispering sail.

Hearts find peace in silent spaces,
Embraced by water's soft graces.
Together here, we drift and dream,
In harmony, a gentle stream.

Navigating through twilight's breath,
Finding solace, embracing death.
In these waters, we are free,
Eternal, boundless, you and me.

Reflections Under the Moonlight

Silver beams on quiet lakes,
Illuminate the paths we take.
Moonlit night, the world asleep,
Secrets whispered, gently seep.

Shadows dance on gentle shores,
Rustling whispers, nature's roars.
Every ripple tells a story,
Of love and loss, of fleeting glory.

Stars above, a million eyes,
Watching dreams as time goes by.
Golden memories intertwined,
In the stillness, hearts align.

Crickets sing their evening song,
Nature hums where we belong.
Drifting thoughts, like clouds above,
Wrapped in peace, cradled in love.

Reflections stir in tranquil pools,
The silent night, a wealth of jewels.
We find ourselves, beneath the light,
In moonlit dreams, all feels right.

Whispers of the Silent Path

Footsteps quiet on a trail,
Nature's breath begins to sail.
Leaves a-shiver in cool shade,
Secrets shared, memories made.

Mossy stones and ancient trees,
Echo softly with the breeze.
Every turn, a story told,
In the whispers, new and old.

Sunlight dapples through the leaves,
Crafting patterns, nature weaves.
In silence, answers gently call,
On this path, we rise and fall.

Beneath the sky, a wider view,
Connecting hearts, just me and you.
In the stillness, we find our way,
Guided by the light of day.

Whispers linger, soft and sweet,
Finding solace, love's heartbeat.
On this silent path we glide,
Together here, side by side.

Echoes in an Empty Chamber

Echoes bounce off barren walls,
Memories trapped in empty halls.
Voices linger, soft and low,
Lost in time, like falling snow.

Shadows play with flickering light,
Haunting whispers in the night.
Each footfall stirs the dust of years,
Revealing laughter, revealing tears.

Time stands still in this old space,
Ghosts of moments we can't replace.
A heavy heart remembers well,
Stories folded in a shell.

Yet within these silent tones,
Hope emerges, even alone.
In the hollow, we find our strength,
Braving echoes at arm's length.

Embrace the void, where silence reigns,
Create anew from past's remains.
In the echoes, life shall flow,
From empty chambers, dreams will grow.

Unraveled Threads of Thought

In the silence, whispers weave,
Fragments lost, yet hard to leave.
Tangled notions, fleeting grace,
A tapestry of time and space.

Scattered dreams upon the floor,
Echoes call from distant shore.
Each thread pulled, a story told,
In the warm embrace of old.

Colors blend, the shadows dance,
A glimpse of fate in every chance.
Ties that bind us, frayed yet bright,
In the chaos, we find light.

Whispers linger, haunting sweet,
In the stillness, hearts will meet.
Unraveled notions softly blend,
Where beginnings meet the end.

Strands of hope, a gentle sigh,
Underneath the vast, wide sky.
Here, the heart finds its refrain,
In the beauty, joy and pain.

Meandering Through Stillness

In the hush where shadows play,
Time stands still, it drifts away.
Mountains sigh, the rivers hum,
Nature whispers, welcome home.

Leaves that dance on softest air,
Every moment, pure and rare.
Footsteps light on ancient ground,
In the quiet, peace is found.

Moonlight bathes the world in gold,
Stories whispered, truths retold.
Pathways weave through dreams untold,
In this stillness, hearts unfold.

Silent nights with stars aglow,
Gentle breezes start to flow.
Every heartbeat softly sways,
In the calm of endless days.

So we wander, hand in hand,
Through the beauty, vast and grand.
Meandering, we find our way,
In the stillness, here we stay.

A Dreamer's Lonesome Expedition

On distant shores where shadows dwell,
A dreamer wanders, seeking well.
With every step, a vision gleams,
In the silence, he chases dreams.

Lonely roads beneath moonlight's glow,
Each heartbeat whispers tales of woe.
He carries hopes in a tattered sack,
A restless spirit, never looking back.

Stars align in a cosmic dance,
Guiding him through fate's expanse.
In the quiet, shadows play,
As dawn breaks, the night gives way.

Voices echo across the plains,
In this solitude, he feels the chains.
Yet every step ignites the flame,
In his heart, he feels no shame.

The horizon calls, an endless blue,
With every breath, he starts anew.
A journey long, yet never done,
In the dreamer's heart, he meets the sun.

Reflections in a Glassy Pool

A mirror smooth beneath the trees,
Holds the secrets of the breeze.
Ripples dance with gentle grace,
As the world reflects its face.

Clouds drift slowly, shadows play,
Sunlight fades at the end of day.
In the depths, the water's sheen,
Holds the stories yet unseen.

Whispers of the past arise,
Echoes calling from the skies.
Time stands still; the heart reveals,
In the stillness, truth conceals.

Every surface tells a tale,
Of silent winds and boats that sail.
In glassy depths, the soul can see,
Moments lost and yet to be.

So kneel beside this tranquil pool,
And listen close; it's nature's school.
In its depth, a world so vast,
Reflections show the present, past.

The Solace of Untold Stories

In shadows deep, where secrets lie,
Whispers weave a tale to sigh.
Pages turn, yet words remain,
A refuge found in quiet pain.

Glimmers of hope in the unspoken,
Hearts find peace in dreams unbroken.
Threads of memories, soft and clear,
A tapestry woven from every tear.

Beneath the stars, a truth unfolds,
Stories linger in the cold.
Each heartbeat echoes, a silent plea,
In every glance, a memory.

The nightingale sings of distant lands,
While the heart whispers, it understands.
Silent oaths beneath the moon,
In solitude, dreams find their tune.

So let the ink flow, soft and slow,
For every story, a place to grow.
In every silence, a world to see,
Embrace the solace of what could be.

Gossamer Trails of Isolation

In quiet rooms where shadows play,
Gossamer threads weave night and day.
Echoes linger in vacant halls,
Each sigh captured as twilight falls.

Fractured whispers float in the air,
Stories barren, hidden despair.
Lonely paths, where footsteps fade,
In solitude's grasp, dreams are laid.

The world outside, a distant hum,
Within these walls, no voices come.
Yet in the silence, a glimmer shines,
Hope dances softly on fragile lines.

A heart's ache wrapped in gentle grace,
Isolation's cloak, a warm embrace.
Yet still the spirit yearns to fly,
To find the warmth beneath the sky.

So trace the patterns, fragile thread,
In each small moment, love is bred.
In gossamer trails, the heart will roam,
Finding strength in the paths unknown.

In the Company of Silence

Silence wraps me like a shawl,
A gentle friend when night does call.
In whispered tones, the darkness speaks,
Finding solace in the peaks.

Stars shine bright, yet softly fade,
In this stillness, fears are laid.
The heart finds rhythm in the hush,
As thoughts uncoil in peaceful rush.

Beneath the moon, shadows grow tall,
In this void, I hear it all.
Every thought, a melody spun,
In solitude, I learn to run.

The quiet cradles dreams at play,
Unraveling truths in the light of day.
In the company of silence, fears dissolve,
Finding the strength to resolve.

So let me linger in this space,
Where quiet moments find their grace.
In stillness, I seek to embrace,
The beauty found in our shared place.

Beneath the Weight of Stillness

In shadows cast by the evening glow,
The weight of silence begins to show.
Each breath a whisper of restless time,
In stillness, my thoughts begin to climb.

The world stands still, a moment drawn,
In gentle hues of jade and dawn.
Restless hearts find solace here,
In the quiet, the truth feels near.

Beneath the weight of every sigh,
Dreams and memories gently fly.
Still waters reflect the skies above,
Caught in the dance of light and love.

Among the stars, a quiet plea,
To carry the weight of what we see.
A gentle echo, a timeless song,
In stillness found, where we belong.

So let me linger where shadows blend,
In this embrace, where time can mend.
Beneath the weight, the heart will find,
The beauty cradled in the mind.

Fragments of a Quiet Heart

In shadows where thoughts gently sway,
Memories linger, softly they play.
Each heartbeat whispers a tale untold,
Of love and loss, of dreams bold.

A delicate dance on the edge of night,
Stars above twinkle, calm and bright.
Pieces of moments, scattered like snow,
Collecting the warmth of what we know.

Silent echoes of laughter remain,
Joys intertwined with threads of pain.
The heart holds fragments, a tender art,
Crafting a canvas from a quiet heart.

In the stillness, secrets unfold,
Stories of bravery, softly retold.
Each sigh a passage, every tear a start,
Building a bridge in a quiet heart.

With every dawn comes a fresh embrace,
A promise of hope, a gentle grace.
All the fragments, once torn apart,
Now form a masterpiece in a quiet heart.

The Path of Whispers

Along the trail where shadows creep,
Soft-spoken secrets begin to leap.
Footprints linger on the dampened ground,
In silence, a thousand truths are found.

Leaves rustle softly, a soothing sound,
Whispers of nature all around.
Each step a heartbeat, a gentle rhyme,
Treading softly, we dance with time.

The wind carries tales from afar,
While twilight wraps us in its shawl.
Paths entwine where souls have been,
In the quiet, the light shines within.

Let the echoes guide where we must roam,
Every whisper, leading us home.
Embracing the journey, as it starts,
On the winding path of whispered arts.

With every dawn, new stories unfold,
Glistening dreams veiled in gold.
Each voice a lantern, lighting the way,
On the path of whispers, come what may.

Dawning Realizations

In the dawn's glow, shadows retreat,
Awakening thoughts, tender and sweet.
The world stirs gently from restful night,
As dreams dissolve in the morning light.

Thoughts cascade like rivers flow,
With clarity found in moments slow.
What once was hidden now clearly shows,
In the heart's quiet, a wisdom grows.

Every sunrise brings forth a chance,
To grasp the day in a hopeful glance.
Lessons learned from paths once crossed,
In the light, we see what was lost.

As new horizons begin to gleam,
We embrace the truth of every dream.
In the stillness, a voice ignites,
Guiding our steps toward lofty heights.

With each dawning, we rise anew,
Facing the world with a clearer view.
Realizations bloom, like flowers bright,
In the soft glow of morning's light.

An Echoing Silence

In the vastness where stillness reigns,
A silence whispers, free from chains.
Echoes bounce in the tranquil air,
Carrying secrets hidden with care.

Moments frozen in gentle embrace,
Time stands still, in this sacred space.
Each breath a story, each sigh a song,
In the echoing silence, we all belong.

Feel the quiet pool beneath our feet,
Where calm and reflection gently meet.
The heartbeats pulse in a rhythmic dance,
In this silence, we find our chance.

Questions flow like a tranquil stream,
In the echoing silence, we dare to dream.
Listen closely to the stillness speak,
In tender moments, the answers peek.

As the world softens, shadows align,
In the depths of silence, the stars will shine.
An echoing calm, a timeless art,
In the stillness, we heal the heart.

In Search of Self

Amidst the whispers of my mind,
I wander paths both dark and kind.
Reflection dances in the night,
Searching for my inner light.

Masks I wear, but who is there?
Each layer stripped, I feel the air.
Shadows fade, I face the truth,
In the silence lies my youth.

Journeys taken, lessons learned,
Through the fire, my spirit burned.
In the mirror, I start to see,
The echo of my soul set free.

Waves of doubt and streams of pain,
Yet through the storm, I break the chain.
With every step, I redefine,
The essence that is truly mine.

In search of self, I roam the land,
With open heart and steady hand.
Each moment holds a chance to be,
The fullest version meant for me.

The Unraveled Map

A parchment crumpled, edges torn,
Leading me to paths forlorn.
With ink that bleeds from time and fate,
I ponder where the lines create.

Mountains rise, rivers flow,
The map reveals where dreams may go.
Yet every turn, a question grows,
What lies beyond the paths that close?

I trace my fingers, feel the thrill,
Every mark a story, every hill.
Yet directions shift like autumn leaves,
And in their dance, my spirit believes.

Compasses spin, wild winds blow,
The journey calls, it's time to go.
With every step, uncertainty,
Yet in the chaos, I am free.

Through tangled woods and starlit skies,
I uncover truths beyond the lies.
For every wrong turn leads to grace,
In uncharted realms, I find my place.

A map unraveled yet refined,
In every lost path, a treasure aligned.
For in this quest, I come to see,
The beauty of the mystery.

Nature's Silent Conversation

Whispers carried on the breeze,
Secrets held in ancient trees.
The rustling leaves, a soft refrain,
Nature speaks where hearts remain.

Streams that glitter in the sun,
Speak of journeys, never done.
In every ripple, tales arise,
Silent thoughts beneath the skies.

Mountains stand like sentinels,
Guardians of the stories' spells.
The echoes call from far and wide,
In nature's arms, we can confide.

Clouds drift lazily, painting dreams,
In their canvas, life redeems.
A rainbow arches, bold and bright,
In every drop, the twinkle of light.

So pause awhile, embrace the sound,
In nature's hush, our truth is found.
For in this quiet, we explore,
The whispers of forevermore.

Breath of the Ether

Inhaled deeply, the world anew,
Each breath a gift, a sacred view.
The ether trembles, pulsates near,
Alive with energy, bright and clear.

A gentle sigh, the universe speaks,
In silence profound, the heart seeks.
Beyond the shackles, love takes flight,
In the stillness, we reach for light.

The ebb and flow of cosmic grace,
In every breath, connected space.
With every inhalation, find,
The whispers of the soul entwined.

Stars aligned in evening's glow,
Breath of the ether starts to flow.
The dance of life, a fragrant breeze,
In harmony, we find our ease.

In quiet moments, lost in thought,
The essence of existence caught.
For in each breath, we are embraced,
By the ether, time and space.

Traces of the Quiet Soul

In shadows deep, whispers grow,
Soft echoes dance, gentle woe.
A heart at peace, a stillness found,
In twilight's grip, no heavy sound.

Footprints linger, soft and light,
Carried forth by winds of night.
Silent thoughts, a tender trace,
Embrace the calm, a warm embrace.

Stars awaken, softly gleam,
Dreams unfold like a quiet stream.
Each moment cherished, held so dear,
In solitude, the soul draws near.

A sigh escapes, a breath in time,
Moments weave in whispered rhyme.
In this realm, the heart can soar,
Exploring depths, forever more.

The night unveils, a sacred space,
Where silence holds a warm grace.
In stillness lies the world's own song,
A quiet place where souls belong.

In the Company of Silence

With every pause, the world fades,
A gentle hush, the heart invades.
In solitude, I find my voice,
The inner calm, my only choice.

Between the beats, a truth revealed,
In whispered dreams, my fate is sealed.
The weight of time, a heavy sigh,
Yet in this space, I learn to fly.

A canvas bare, where thoughts take flight,
Lonely stars shine through the night.
In every breath, a story weaves,
In silence, love and hope receives.

The quiet hum of nature calls,
In hidden nooks, where silence falls.
Each moment swells, a timeless blend,
In this embrace, the soul ascends.

Echoes dance on cool night air,
Solitude, my only care.
Among the stillness, I reside,
In the warmth of silence, I abide.

The Breath of Alone

Beneath the stars, I find my ground,
In every breath, solitude's sound.
The world spins on, a distant tune,
While I embrace the silver moon.

In shadows cast, I draw my breath,
Woven through whispers of life and death.
Each exhale, a piece of me,
In quietude, I learn to be.

The night unveils, a soft refrain,
Here in the dark, I feel no pain.
A gentle pulse, a soothing balm,
In the heart of night, I find my calm.

Paths of silence branch and twine,
In solitude, the world aligns.
Each moment stretches, time stands still,
In this embrace, I find my will.

The breath of alone, sweet and pure,
A guiding light, forever sure.
In stillness found, my spirit glows,
Through every silence, wisdom grows.

Murmurs of an Untold Tale

In hidden corners, stories hide,
Whispered tales, where dreams abide.
Each murmur soft, a world unfolds,
Layers deep, with secrets told.

The echoes linger, faint and shy,
As shadows dance beneath the sky.
In silence, stories seek their way,
A journey born from hidden day.

With every heartbeat, a voice awakes,
In quiet moments, fate remakes.
A tapestry, woven with care,
Murmurs call from everywhere.

In twilight's grasp, we gather round,
With gentle peace, our hearts unbound.
Untold moments share a glance,
In hushed embrace, we find our chance.

The night brings forth, a timeless grace,
Each whispered story finds its place.
In murmur soft, the truth prevails,
Within the heart, untold tales sail.

Where Shadows Rest

In the quiet glen where whispers play,
The gentle dusk greets the fading day.
Beneath the arch of the ancient trees,
Lies the calm where time bends with ease.

Cool breezes brush the twilight air,
Bringing secrets without a care.
The shadows stretch and softly blend,
In this place where the light must end.

Flickering fireflies dance in the gloom,
Casting soft spells beneath the moon.
Nature holds her breath in grace,
As darkness wraps this tranquil place.

Memories linger in the fading light,
Echoes of laughter fade into night.
In the stillness, dreams intertwine,
Where time is soft, and hearts align.

Here in the hush where the shadows rest,
Peace settles deep within the chest.
As stars awaken in skies so vast,
A gentle reminder of moments past.

Solitary Horizons

A quiet shore meets the endless sea,
Whispers of dreams call out to me.
Waves caress the sands so fine,
Where solitude and solace entwine.

Endless skies cradle the setting sun,
Painting the world where journeys run.
Footprints vanish with the evening tide,
In the vastness, I learn to abide.

Clouds drift slowly, soft as a sigh,
Mirroring thoughts that wander high.
Every horizon holds a new tale,
One that beckons, one that will sail.

Amidst the silence, I find my way,
Navigating dreams that sway and play.
Each horizon brings a different view,
A canvas painted in shades of blue.

In this solitude, I cultivate peace,
Embracing the stillness that will not cease.
The horizon whispers, a promise true,
In the heart's embrace, I start anew.

Solitude in Bloom

In the garden where the wildflowers grow,
Petals unfold in a gentle show.
Colors burst like thoughts in the mind,
Reminders of beauty, so hard to find.

Bees hum softly, weaving through air,
A dance of existence, tender and rare.
In this solitude, I'm never alone,
Nature surrounds me, a welcoming home.

Morning dew glistens like tiny stars,
Transforming the earth with delicate bars.
Each breath I take is sweet and light,
In the embrace of the growing night.

Time lingers still within this space,
Nature's art brings a soothing grace.
Among the blooms, my spirit takes flight,
In this haven of peace, all feels right.

Solitude whispers in fragrant tones,
Cocooned in beauty, I find my own.
With every petal, I learn to believe,
In the magic of stillness, I truly receive.

The Sound of One's Voice

In a crowded room, silence sings loud,
A lone heart breaks from within the crowd.
Whispers of hope fade into the night,
While dreams echo softly, yearning for light.

Thoughts spiral like leaves in the breeze,
Seeking a moment of comfort and ease.
The sound of one's voice can change the air,
A melody woven with heartfelt care.

Notes stretch and bend, like shadows at dusk,
Filling the void with warmth, like a husk.
Each word a bridge to the hidden soul,
A chance to unite, to make one whole.

In the stillness, courage finds its tone,
A voice raised high breaks through the alone.
Every story shared, a thread in the whole,
Weaving connections that empower the soul.

The sound of one's voice, a gentle guide,
In the cacophony where hearts collide.
Finding strength in the quietest place,
Echoing truth with a tender embrace.

Lost in the Quiet Woods

Amidst the trees, a whisper calls,
The rustling leaves, where silence falls.
Footsteps soft on the mossy ground,
Nature's peace, a soothing sound.

Branches sway, a gentle dance,
Sunlight gleams, a fleeting glance.
In this realm, my worries cease,
Wrapped in shadows, I find my peace.

Birds above in leisurely flight,
Chasing dreams in fading light.
Here, the heart learns to be free,
Lost within this tranquil sea.

Time flows slow, the world obscured,
In each breath, my soul's assured.
With every step, an echo sings,
Of hidden truths, of sacred things.

A journey deep, where thoughts entwine,
Lost in the woods, my spirit aligns.
Nature's grace, my gentle guide,
Here in the quiet, I bide my stride.

Silent Conversations with the Soul

In the stillness, whispers rise,
Thoughts emerge beneath the skies.
Silhouettes of dreams entwined,
In quietude, my heart is aligned.

Words unspoken, yet so clear,
Embrace the calm, release the fear.
Time suspended, moments blend,
In this refuge, I transcend.

Echoes dance in the twilight glow,
Simplicity, the treasures we sow.
With every sigh, a truth revealed,
In silence deep, our fate is sealed.

Remnants linger of days long past,
Lessons learned, shadows cast.
Here, the heart remembers well,
In silent talks, I break the shell.

The soul listens, the mind takes flight,
In the quiet, the world feels right.
Silent conversations weave the thread,
Connecting all, where I am led.

Crickets and the Weight of Stillness

Crickets chirp in the velvet night,
A symphony of pure delight.
Stars above, a glimmering view,
Waves of silence, calm and true.

The night wraps around, a heavy cloak,
In every pause, a story spoke.
Nature holds its breath in grace,
Time seems to slow, we find our place.

The air is thick, yet lightly flows,
In the dark, a secret grows.
The weight of stillness, heavy yet light,
Whispers linger in the night.

Beneath the moon, a dance unfolds,
Of wishes made and hopes retold.
Crickets play their nightly tune,
A melody beneath the moon.

In the quiet, spirits rise,
Lost in dreams beneath the skies.
The weight of stillness, soft and bold,
Crickets sing of tales untold.

Seeking Truth in Solitude

In the silence, my heart takes flight,
Boundless thoughts in the blanket of night.
A journey deep within my mind,
In solitude, the truth I find.

Mountains high, valleys low,
In quiet moments, the spirit grows.
Words unspoken, yet so profound,
In the stillness, wisdoms abound.

Echoes of a life lived true,
In every shadow, a deeper view.
Embracing fears, I walk alone,
In solitude, I find my home.

The world outside may rush and race,
But here, I find my sacred space.
Seeking truth, the heart will soar,
In solitude, I seek for more.

A tapestry of thoughts laid bare,
In quiet whispers, I find my prayer.
Each heartbeat sings a timeless song,
In solitude, I feel I belong.

A Trail of Stillness

In the woods where shadows play,
Whispers dance in soft array.
Leaves flutter gently, secrets keep,
Nature's hush invites the deep.

Footsteps light on earthy ground,
Filling silence, sweetly found.
Every breath a soothing balm,
Surrounding peace, a quiet calm.

Mossy stones and winding streams,
Carry dreams, and ancient themes.
Branches arch, like arms they sway,
Guiding hearts that drift away.

Sunlight fades, the dusk arrives,
In twilight's grasp, the spirit thrives.
A trail of stillness, soft and bright,
Leads us gently into night.

In the Company of Dusk

The sun bows low, a painter's brush,
With strokes of gold, in quiet hush.
Sky wears a cloak of pastel hue,
As day whispers its soft adieu.

Shadows stretch, and crickets sing,
A melody of evening's wing.
Streetlights flicker, one by one,
A dance beneath the setting sun.

In the company of dusk, we find,
A moment's peace for heart and mind.
Breathe in the cool, the calming air,
Embrace the night without a care.

Stars awaken in the deepening sky,
Guiding lost souls who wander by.
Their twinkle tells of dreams that soar,
In the company of dusk, we explore.

Quiet Musings Under Stars

Under a blanket stitched with light,
Thoughts drift softly into the night.
The cosmos hums a gentle tune,
While hearts gather beneath the moon.

Each flicker holds a tale untold,
Of lovers lost, of spirits bold.
Silent echoes of wishes made,
In night's embrace, our fears do fade.

Clouds weave stories with silver thread,
In this vast dome, our dreams are fed.
We dance in timeless cosmic play,
With quiet musings leading our way.

Moments linger, soft and rare,
In the stillness, life feels bare.
Yet in that emptiness we find,
A universe alive, combined.

The Solace in Absence

In absence lies a quiet grace,
An echo of a cherished space.
Silence speaks in softest tones,
Filling gaps where love still roams.

Memories wrap like morning mist,
Each thought a tender, gentle kiss.
Time stands still, yet moves along,
An unseen thread still holds us strong.

A breeze may stir, a sign you're near,
In whispered sighs, I feel you here.
The stars align in patterns bright,
Reminding me of our shared light.

Absence holds what words can't say,
In heartbeats, we find our way.
The solace found in what remains,
Is love's sweet echo, free from chains.

Shadows of Reflection

In twilight's glow the shadows dance,
Thoughts flicker like leaves in chance.
Reflections whisper tales untold,
In depths of silence, secrets unfold.

Eyes cast down, the world feels far,
Memories drift like a distant star.
Echoes linger where dreams once played,
In the arms of night, fears often stayed.

The mirror speaks in fractured lines,
A truth concealed where hope intertwines.
Shadows stretch, embrace the light,
In their fold, we learn to fight.

Lessons taught by the fading sun,
Each moment savored, each battle won.
In reflection, a heart finds peace,
In the quiet glow, sorrows cease.

So let the shadows softly sway,
Guiding souls along their way.
With every step, a chance to grow,
In shadows of reflection, we learn to flow.

Whispers of the Lonely Road

Along the path where echoes sigh,
Whispers dance on breezes high.
Footsteps falter, hearts stand still,
In solitude, dreams start to fill.

Each twist and turn, a story weaves,
Underneath the autumn leaves.
A mile marked by shadows cast,
The past remembers, holding fast.

Stars above shine with quiet grace,
Illuminating this empty space.
The road ahead, a silent friend,
In whispers shared, the heart will mend.

With every step, a tale untold,
Of courage found in moments bold.
The lonely road, a sacred song,
Where we discover where we belong.

And as the night begins to fade,
Hope rises where fears were laid.
On this journey, we find the way,
In whispers of the road, we stay.

Where Silence Meets the Heart

In the stillness, time unwinds,
Softly echoing the peace it finds.
Where silence breathes, the heart can hear,
A melody that draws us near.

Words unspoken, yet understood,
In the quiet, we find the good.
The pulse of life, a gentle beat,
In silence, we feel complete.

Moments linger, suspended in grace,
Where worries fade and dreams embrace.
The heart awakens to tender thoughts,
In the sanctuary silence brought.

Reflections glimmer in muted light,
Guiding us through the veil of night.
A sacred pause, an open space,
Where silence and heart find their place.

So let us cherish these still, small hours,
In silence, we bloom like blossomed flowers.
For in the quiet, life's truths impart,
Residing sweetly, where silence meets the heart.

Solitude's Embrace

In the quiet of the evening's glow,
Solitude wraps its gentle flow.
A soft caress, a tender muse,
In stillness found, we cannot lose.

The world outside fades far away,
In solitude, we choose to stay.
Thoughts like rivers softly stream,
Flowing through the heart's deep dream.

With every breath, a new release,
A journey inward, finding peace.
In solitude, our spirits soar,
Embracing what we long for more.

Branches sway in the evening breeze,
Whispered secrets through the trees.
In this embrace, we're never alone,
For within, we find our home.

So let the night unfold its grace,
In solitude's embrace, we find our place.
In quiet moments, life's beauty glows,
A peaceful heart is how love grows.

Solitary Sunshine

A beam breaks through the clouds above,
Chasing shadows, whispering love.
It warms the earth, a gentle touch,
In solitude, it means so much.

Golden rays dance on the brook,
In nature's embrace, I find a nook.
The world fades away, a fleeting glance,
In this moment, I lose my stance.

Birds sing sweetly, a morning hymn,
The light grows strong, no place for dim.
Around me blooms a garden bright,
In solitude, all feels just right.

I wander forth on winding trails,
Where laughter scatters, joy prevails.
Through fields of gold and skies of blue,
The sun alone feels so true.

As day drifts softly into night,
The stars arise, a wondrous sight.
In solitude, my heart will shine,
A sacred space where love entwines.

Where Time Stands Still

In whispers soft, the moments freeze,
A gentle hush, the world at ease.
Here time unwinds, a quiet thrill,
In stillness found, my heart is still.

The clock hands pause, a sacred space,
I find my peace, embrace the grace.
With every breath, the silence grows,
In tranquil depths, the stillness flows.

Nature holds its breath in awe,
A canvas brushed with a perfect flaw.
Each leaf, each stone, a story tells,
In this realm where magic dwells.

I linger long, my soul takes flight,
In shadows cast by fading light.
Where dreamers wish and lovers sigh,
In timeless realms, we learn to fly.

As stars emerge, the night ignites,
In deep embrace, my spirit ignites.
Where time stands still, forever calls,
In silent whispers, the heart enthralls.

A Symphony of One

In solitude, the music flows,
A symphony that gently grows.
Each note a step upon the path,
In quiet grace, I find my math.

The strings resonate, the woodwinds sigh,
In harmony, my spirit flies.
A single voice, so strong and clear,
In solitude, I hold it dear.

The world around fades into sound,
In every heartbeat, I am found.
A dance of thoughts, a rhythmic sway,
In symphony, I lose the day.

With every pause, I feel the call,
The echo swells, it wraps us all.
A melody that knows no end,
In solitude, I learn to blend.

A symphony of one, I sing,
In quietude, my heart takes wing.
With every breath, the world I weave,
In solitude, I dare believe.

Echoes of Solitary Echoes

In empty halls, the echoes play,
Whispers of thoughts that drift away.
A haunting song, a soft refrain,
In solitude, I feel the strain.

The silence speaks in tones of gray,
Where shadows linger and hearts sway.
Each echo dances through the night,
In solitude, I seek the light.

Memories rise like morning mist,
In fleeting dreams, I find the tryst.
The past resounds, a call so clear,
In solitude, I hold it near.

A cycle spun through time and space,
In echoes, I find my place.
The past and present, hand in hand,
In solitude, I learn to stand.

As dawn awakens, silence fades,
Echoes linger in the glades.
In solitude, I've come to see,
It's here, in stillness, I am free.

Lighthouses of Thought

In the fog, they stand tall,
Guiding ships through the night.
Wisdom shines from the heights,
Beacons of soft, steady light.

Each ray a whisper of hope,
Illuminating the path found.
In minds where dreams roam free,
A sanctuary of thought profound.

With every turn of the tide,
New ideas come to play.
Casting doubts far away,
In these lighthouses we stay.

The waves may crash and roar,
But steadfast, they hold true.
In a world of shifting sands,
Thought lighthouses shine through.

So sail forth with courage,
Navigating with trust and care.
For within each beacon's glow,
A treasure of knowledge is there.

The Light of Isolation

In silence, shadows creep,
Where whispers find their home.
A solitary journey,
In thoughts we often roam.

Loneliness weaves a tale,
Of nights beneath the stars.
Yet in this quiet space,
A glow can mend the scars.

Shadows dance on the walls,
In patterns all their own.
Each flicker tells a story,
Of the heart's hidden throne.

Isolation's tender glow,
Can spark a flame inside.
A chance to learn and grow,
In stillness, we confide.

As dawn breaks through the dark,
The light connects us all.
Even in solitude's grip,
Together, we stand tall.

Beyond the Veil of Silence

In whispers soft as air,
Secrets linger in the night.
Beneath the veil of silence,
Is a world of hidden light.

Echoes of what once was,
Drift like leaves on the ground.
Stories waiting to be told,
In silence, they are found.

Beyond the stillness, breath deep,
A symphony of unseen grace.
Every pause a memory,
In time's warm embrace.

What lies beyond the hush,
Is beauty yet to bloom.
In the heart of quietude,
Resides a fragrant room.

So listen to the silence,
Let it envelop your soul.
For in the peace we discover,
A stillness makes us whole.

Chasing Shadows Alone

In twilight's gentle arms,
I wander on my own.
Chasing shadows in the dusk,
Fleeting moments, overthrown.

Each shape a story untold,
A flicker of what used to be.
Through the labyrinth of dreams,
Whispers guide me, set me free.

Steps echo on the ground,
In a dance with the setting sun.
On this road of nothings,
The chase has just begun.

Solitude is my companion,
Through the dark, I stride.
Finding peace in the chase,
With shadows as my guide.

As night drapes its curtain,
The pursuit deepens still.
In hollow echoes of laughter,
Chasing shadows, I find my will.

Solitary Stars in a Vast Sky

In the hush of night, they gleam so bright,
Whispers of dreams take flight.
Each one holds a tale untold,
In the expanse, so brave and bold.

Winking like secrets, far away,
Guiding the lost who stray.
A tapestry of glimmering dust,
In the cosmos, we trust.

They dance in silence, a cosmic show,
Eternal embers, soft and slow.
In solitude, they find their grace,
In the skies, their destined place.

Fleeting moments, a fleeting glow,
Infinite wonders, forever flow.
Solitary yet never alone,
In the vastness, perfectly grown.

They beckon the hearts of the dreamers,
In the dark, they are beacons.
Stars that shimmer, guide and inspire,
Setting within us a longing desire.

Wandering Among Shadows

In the twilight, shadows creep,
Whispers linger, secrets keep.
Footsteps tread on silent ground,
In the dark, solace is found.

Echoes wander through the trees,
Carried softly by the breeze.
Moonlit paths reveal the way,
As night transforms into day.

Flickering lanterns, faint and dim,
Guiding spirits, frail and grim.
Among the shades, a figure sways,
Lost in the twilight haze.

Dreams entwined with silken night,
Veiled in mystery, soft and light.
Every shadow tells a tale,
In their embrace, we shall not fail.

Wandering hearts in quiet thrall,
Answering the night's soft call.
In shadows deep, our spirits soar,
Finding solace forevermore.

A Dance with Quietude

In the stillness, whispers play,
Gentle moments drift away.
Nature's breath, a soothing balm,
In quietude, we find our calm.

Softly now the twilight glows,
In peace, our inner rhythm flows.
A dance of thoughts, both light and deep,
In silence, treasures we reap.

Stars above join in the trance,
Creating space for a gentle dance.
With every breath, we learn to sway,
In the quiet, we find our way.

The heartbeats echo, true and slow,
In the depths, our spirits grow.
A twirl, a spin, a soft embrace,
In stillness, time holds its grace.

Together in this sacred space,
We melt into the night's embrace.
With quietude, forever blessed,
In this dance, our souls find rest.

The Road Less Spoken

Amidst the noise, a path unfolds,
Whispers of wonders, yet untold.
With every step, the heart takes flight,
On the road where dreams ignite.

The branches wave, a silent cheer,
Embracing tales both far and near.
Where journeys cross, and shadows blend,
On this road, time has no end.

Footprints etched in forgotten soil,
Each turn and twist, a tale of toil.
The echoes guide, though scarcely heard,
In silence, we find the unspoken word.

With courage bold, we walk alone,
In the mystery, seeds are sown.
Life's tapestry we weave with grace,
On the road of our own embrace.

Through valleys deep and hills that rise,
We chase the sun, we touch the skies.
The road less spoken calls us near,
In its embrace, we lose our fear.

Beneath the Canopy of Solitude

In the quiet grove where shadows play,
Whispers dance in the softest sway.
Leaves murmur secrets of bygone years,
In this hush, the heart feels no fears.

Branches weave a tapestry above,
Cocooned in nature's gentle love.
Moonlight spills like a silver stream,
Filling the night with a tranquil dream.

Footsteps light on the forest floor,
Each step a promise, an open door.
Here in the thicket, time stands still,
A sanctuary for the wandering will.

Beneath the boughs, the world's disdain,
Fades like echoes in gentle rain.
Solitude cradles the weary soul,
In its embrace, we become whole.

With every sigh, the night expands,
Caressing silence with tender hands.
Beneath the canopy, we find our way,
In solitude's arms, forever we stay.

The Lullaby of Unseen Horizons

In the twilight glow, dreams take flight,
A lullaby calls in the softest night.
Waves of silence crash on the shore,
Whispers of wonders we can explore.

Stars twinkle bright like secrets kept,
In the canvas of night, our wishes leapt.
Each twinkling spark a tale to share,
Of journeys begun, of hearts laid bare.

Beyond the hills, where shadows blend,
Horizons beckon with promises to mend.
In the hush of night, love's echoes ring,
A gentle reminder of what dreams bring.

The moon's embrace lights the hidden path,
Guiding our steps with a soothing wran.
Each pause a breath, each sigh a sigh,
In the lullaby's arms, we learn to fly.

The unseen beckons, a world untold,
In the heart of night's warmth, we are bold.
With every heartbeat, we dare to see,
Unseen horizons that set us free.

Mapping the Inner Wilderness

In the depths of thought where shadows dwell,
Maps are drawn where the wild hearts swell.
Paths of feeling cross and ignite,
Leading us toward our inner light.

Canyons of doubt and mountains of fear,
We chart our way, though the end's not clear.
With ink of courage, we sketch our tale,
In the wilderness where the brave prevail.

Every turn uncertain, yet beckoning bright,
A compass of hope shines through the night.
We discover treasures in unmarked trails,
In the wild of our hearts, adventure prevails.

Rivers of thought meander and flow,
Carving a place where rawness can grow.
With every heartbeat, we claim our ground,
In the rich tapestry of life, we're found.

Mapping the wild, we find our way,
Through canyons of longing, we learn to sway.
For in the inner wilderness we see,
The beauty of being, of simply being free.

Footsteps on Untrodden Ground

Every step we take is a mark we leave,
On untrodden ground, we learn to believe.
With hearts wide open, we head into unknown,
In the quiet of dawn, seeds of courage are sown.

The earth holds stories, rich and profound,
In its tender embrace, our hopes are unbound.
We wander with purpose, not seeking a map,
Finding our way in this life's gentle lap.

Fallen leaves whisper of paths yet to tread,
In the echoes of nature, our fears are shed.
Each footprint a promise, each breath a song,
On untrodden ground, we finally belong.

With every horizon that calls out our name,
We chase the whispers, igniting the flame.
For in the silence, we hear the sound,
Of dreams unfolding on untrodden ground.

So let us walk boldly, hand in hand,
Through valleys and peaks, across every land.
In the journey of life, let our spirits soar,
Footsteps on untrodden ground forevermore.

Reflections in Still Water

Beneath the sky, the water lies,
A mirror framed by whispering trees.
Moments captured in soft sighs,
Nature holds her secrets with ease.

Ripples dance, then fade away,
Time slips past in gentle grace.
Clouds above join in the play,
Painting shadows on this face.

Fishes dart, a fleeting glance,
The world distills in silken hues.
In this calm, I find my chance,
To ponder life, to muse and choose.

The sun dips low, gold spills like wine,
A tranquil glow on tranquil lands.
Here at dusk, all is divine,
Reflections held in silent hands.

As night unfolds its velvet cloak,
Stars emerge, a distant song.
In this space, my heart awoke,
In stillness, I forever belong.

Winds of the Unheard

In the quiet, secrets sigh,
Winds carry tales we cannot hear.
Whispers brush against the sky,
Echoes linger, drawing near.

Leaves tremble in the gentle breath,
Nature's voice, both soft and strong.
Beyond the silence, whispers death,
Yet in the stillness, life beats on.

Winds weave through the hidden paths,
Caressing all that dare to grow.
In shadows deep, the essence laughs,
For time will tell what we don't know.

Each gust a story, each gust a plea,
Tales of love, of loss, of dreams.
In every swirl, the timeless sea,
Flows beneath our silent screams.

So chase the winds, but heed them well,
For in their flight, there lies a clue.
To dance with fate, to rise and fell,
The unheard winds will guide you through.

The Dance of No One

In empty rooms where shadows play,
The echoes roam with silent grace.
Each corner holds a faded sway,
An unseen partner in this space.

No witness here to keep the time,
Just whispers in the dusky air.
The heartbeats pulse, a secret rhyme,
In simple steps, we shed our care.

Footprints fade upon the floor,
As if they never left a trace.
Yet passion's twirl forevermore,
Enfolds the void in soft embrace.

The moonlight casts a silver glow,
Choreography of night's design.
In stillness, energy will flow,
A dance of dreams, both yours and mine.

So twirl in spaces void of light,
Where no one sees the dance unfold.
In solitude, we find our flight,
A timeless art, a story told.

An Empty Canvas

Before me lies a space untold,
Whispers of color beg for release.
Each brush awaits to break the mold,
To weave in moments, find my peace.

With every stroke, a tale combines,
A dance of hues beneath my hand.
Imagination softly twines,
Creating realms that brightly stand.

The canvas breathes, alive and wide,
Emotions clash and softly blend.
Here in this zone, my soul confides,
Every line a truth, a friend.

Splash of blue, a dash of red,
Colors sing in harmony's grace.
In every corner, dreams are fed,
In this vast space, I find my place.

So let the silence guide the flow,
Each line a journey, bold and free.
On this canvas, I will grow,
In each creation, I will see.

Wandering in Silence

In twilight's glow, where shadows blend,
The whispers of the wind ascend.
A solemn path, with secrets vast,
I tread on dreams of ages past.

Beneath the stars, my thoughts take flight,
Wrapped in the cloak of the cool night.
The world fades soft, but I remain,
A quiet heart, untouched by pain.

The rustle of leaves, a gentle song,
In this stillness, I belong.
Each step I take, the earth replies,
In silent ways, where wisdom lies.

Time hangs suspended, moments freeze,
In nature's arms, my spirit sees.
As echoes fade into the mist,
I find the peace that I had wished.

And as I wander, lost yet found,
In silence, love and hope abound.
The journey ends where it began,
In quietude, I understand.

Echoes of the Untouched Path

Upon the trail where few have walked,
In nature's realm, deep thoughts are locked.
The echoes call, a distant sound,
Where ancient trees and dreams are crowned.

The butterflies dance, like fleeting thoughts,
In sunlit glades, where time is caught.
Each step reveals the wonders vast,
A wandering spirit, free at last.

With every turn, a story dwells,
The hidden truths the forest tells.
The sunlight breaks through leafy crowns,
Upon this path, my heart resounds.

The whispering winds, the rustling leaves,
A symphony that nature weaves.
In solitude, my soul takes flight,
Embraced by shadows, kissed by light.

As I trek forth, the world ignites,
With every step, new worlds invite.
In echoes soft, my heart aligns,
With untold stories nature finds.

Footsteps in Quietude

Gentle whispers greet the dawn,
In quietude, I walk alone.
With every footfall, peace I seek,
The heart speaks softly, never weak.

The path unfolds beneath my feet,
Each step a rhythm, steady beat.
The morning dew, a fleeting gift,
As nature's hand begins to lift.

Sunlight dapples through the trees,
A tranquil breeze, a sweet release.
In silent moments, truths appear,
The world is vast, yet crystal clear.

With shadows long and whispers low,
I find the light that begins to glow.
In solitude, I learn to see,
The beauty in simplicity.

This quiet path, my heart's embrace,
With every step, I find my place.
A journey inward, winding slow,
Footsteps in quietude, I know.

The Solitary Trail

Along the solitary trail I roam,
Beneath the sky, my heart finds home.
Each moment lingers, soft and bright,
A world unveiled in fading light.

The call of birds in morning air,
Awakens dreams, both bold and rare.
With every turn, I feel a spark,
A silent guide through light and dark.

Reflections dance on shimmering streams,
In nature's arms, I weave my dreams.
A symphony of quiet grace,
In solitude, I find my place.

The frozen leaves beneath my feet,
Whisper stories of those I meet.
In gentle murmurs, nature speaks,
In hushed tones, the spirit seeks.

So onward, onward, without fear,
On this trail, my purpose clear.
In solitude, I learn and grow,
The solitary trail, my soul's echo.

The Stillness Within

In the hush before dawn's light,
Whispers stir in the quiet night.
A soft breeze plays through the trees,
Bringing peace like a gentle tease.

Thoughts drift like leaves on a stream,
Floating softly in a fragile dream.
Moments linger, time stands still,
Calmness wraps like a warm, soft quilt.

Beneath the surface, echoes dwell,
Secrets of the heart, they swell.
In solitude, shadows dance,
Waiting for the dawn's advance.

Every heartbeat, a silent song,
Against the world, it feels so wrong.
Yet in this place, courage grows,
The stillness reveals what one truly knows.

Hope is whispered through the dark,
A flicker of light, a kindling spark.
In the stillness, we find our truth,
A quiet strength, ageless as youth.

Pathways of the Mind

In the corridors of thought, I roam,
Seeking answers, carving a home.
The maps I trace are made of dreams,
Where light and shadow dance in streams.

Footsteps echo on the floor of time,
Each decision, a subtle rhyme.
Along the paths where musings flow,
Ideas blossom, and wild winds blow.

Winding roads, both bold and bare,
Take me to places steeped in air.
Through tangled vines of memory's weave,
I find solace, I dare to believe.

Moments collide, like stars in flight,
Each one dancing, drawing me tight.
In this maze where thoughts intertwine,
I uncover the brilliance of the divine.

The journey unfolds, feet find their grace,
In every quirk, in every space.
Pathways may twist, but hearts stay true,
Navigating the vastness, we break through.

Untold Tales of the Lost

In shadows deep, where secrets lie,
Whispers of stories long goodbye.
Each echo holds a fleeting sigh,
Of dreams unspoken, of reasons why.

Wanderers tread on forgotten ground,
In silence, their hopes are tightly wound.
A tapestry woven with threads of pain,
In the silence, legacy remains.

Beneath the stars, their voices wail,
Recounting journeys, a ghostly trail.
Each heart a story, a world unseen,
Sacred and lost in the in-between.

Through haunted woods, in silence lost,
A testament to the heavy cost.
Yet in the dark, embers still glow,
From ashes buried, new dreams grow.

Listen close, and you may hear,
The whispers of those we hold dear.
For every tale that's lost in time,
Finds its place in a hidden rhyme.

Solitary Reflections

By the window, a world unfolds,
Silhouetted stories left untold.
In solitude, I find my grace,
In the quiet, I embrace my space.

The mirror shows a face unknown,
Layers peeled, truths are grown.
Eyes speak softly, in deep regard,
Unraveling fears, life is hard.

Clouds drift lazily, thoughts like birds,
Freedom found in unspoken words.
Whispers of time wrap round my heart,
Each moment savored, a work of art.

In stillness, I ponder the night,
Embracing darkness, welcoming light.
Reflections dance on the water's skin,
And in this place, I begin to begin.

So here I sit, with all I've sought,
Embracing the lessons life has taught.
In solitude, I am not alone,
In every silence, I have grown.

Under the Veil of Quietude

A whisper hides in shadows deep,
Where secrets of the heart still keep.
The world outside fades to a hum,
In tranquil moments, I become.

The stars above begin to gleam,
In stillness, I weave a gentle dream.
Time drifts slow like evening tide,
Wrapped in peace where thoughts can hide.

Each breath a note in silence played,
A symphony in twilight laid.
Under this veil, I find my peace,
In soft serenity, worries cease.

The shadows dance on walls of night,
Soft lanterns glow, casting light.
Beneath the veil, my spirit soars,
In quietude, my heart explores.

In solitude's embrace, I'm free,
Lost in dreams, just me and me.
The world can wait while I reside,
Under the veil, my calm, my guide.

Driftwood Thoughts

Upon a shore where dreams are found,
Driftwood thoughts gather 'round.
Each piece a story, washed by time,
In nature's rhythm, I find my rhyme.

The ocean whispers secrets low,
As tides of memory ebb and flow.
Carved signs of life float ashore,
Each a reminder, forevermore.

With every wave, reflections swell,
In drifts of wood, I hear them tell.
The echoes of laughter, sighs of grace,
Stretch across this familiar place.

I wander through the pieces strewn,
Beneath the fickle, watchful moon.
In every grain, a tale is sown,
In driftwood thoughts, I'm never alone.

The ocean's heart, a timeless friend,
In currents deep, where dreams suspend.
Each fleeting thought, a fleeting wave,
In driftwood's arms, my spirit's saved.

Navigating the Silent Sea

In twilight hours when shadows play,
I set my sails where dreams relay.
The silent sea, an open door,
Calls with whispers to explore.

The stars align, my compass guides,
Through tranquil waters where time abides.
Each ripple whispers tales untold,
In the depths of night, a courage bold.

With every stroke, the stillness sings,
A harmony of soft, gentle things.
The moon reflects upon my path,
Navigating calm, away from wrath.

In solitude, I find my strength,
Embracing journeys of great length.
While silence wraps its arms around,
The world's sweet peace is found.

Through tempered waves and starlit skies,
My heart finds solace; it never lies.
Navigating dreams without a care,
In this silent sea, I discover air.

Threads of Solitude

In the loom of life, threads intertwine,
Simple moments, a tapestry fine.
In solitude, I stitch and weave,
Creating patterns, quietly believe.

Each thread a thought, an echo slight,
A single whisper in the night.
Colors dance like sunlight's kiss,
In solitude, I find my bliss.

The needle glides, a soft embrace,
Weaving memories, tracing space.
Through quiet hours, I learn to see,
The beauty found in just being me.

Patterns form with gentle grace,
In solitude, I carve my place.
Each silent moment softly calls,
In threads of solitude, my spirit sprawls.

So here I stay, in this gentle art,
Weaving dreams that fill my heart.
With every stitch, I come alive,
In threads of solitude, I thrive.

The Void Between Us

In shadows we linger, the silence grows,
A chasm of whispers, where no one knows.
The echoes of laughter, now distant and faint,
Paint pictures of moments, where love was innate.

Your gaze drifts away, lost in the night,
While I reach for stars, keeping hope in sight.
Yet time spins a web, too tangled to part,
Leaving a void where you once held my heart.

In dreams, we still dance through the empty air,
Two figures entwined, though you're never there.
The space in-between feels both heavy and light,
As I yearn for your warmth in the cold of the night.

Memories linger like shadows of mist,
Fleeting reminders of moments we kissed.
I whisper your name to the silenced moon,
In the void that's become a haunting tune.

Yet still in this silence, there's beauty I find,
A resilience forged, in the depths of the mind.
For love can't dissolve, though the distance is vast,
In the void, it remains, an eternal contrast.

Alone with the Stars

Beneath the vast sky, the stars start to glow,
A tapestry woven where dreams gently flow.
I sit in the silence, the world far away,
Lost in the magic of the end of the day.

Each twinkle a whisper, a promise of light,
Guiding my heart through the velvet of night.
I sigh with the moon, my companion so dear,
Together we float on the waves of the sphere.

The universe watches, a canvas divine,
Painting my sorrows, transforming to shine.
In solitude's grasp, I find solace and peace,
With stars as my friends, my worries release.

Though darkness surrounds me, I learn to embrace,
The beauty of stillness, the calmness of space.
In this gentle moment, I'm never alone,
For the stars are my family, the night is my home.

So here I'll remain, as the night drapes its wares,
With the cosmos above, I shed all my cares.
Embracing the wonder, I let my heart soar,
Alone with the stars, forever explore.

Memories on the Wind

Whispers of laughter float through the air,
A gentle reminder of moments we share.
The breeze carries stories, both tender and light,
Of days filled with joy, now lost to the night.

Leaves rustle softly, like echoes of cheer,
Replaying the memories that brought us so near.
Each breath of the wind holds the past in its sway,
As I chase the fond moments that drift far away.

The sun paints the sky with colors so bold,
Like brushstrokes of dreams from the stories we're told.
With each gust, I feel, the time has been kind,
As I gather the treasures that drift with the wind.

Yet shadows of sorrow whisper a tune,
That mingles with laughter beneath the soft moon.
I dance with the thoughts of the past that I knew,
With memories on the wind, forever true.

And though time rolls on, like the waves on the sea,
I'll cherish each heartbeat, each fragment of thee.
For the winds carry tales, both fragile and grand,
Of love that was woven by the gentle hand.

A Canvas of Quiet Moments

In stillness we breathe, the world fades away,
Each second a brushstroke, in shades of the day.
A canvas of quiet, where hearts gently speak,
In whispers of insight, it's solace we seek.

The sun dips low, painting shadows and light,
As silence embraces the coming of night.
With colors of twilight that softly expand,
Moments of peace in the warmth of your hand.

Around us a symphony, soft as a sigh,
The rustle of leaves, the brightening sky.
We carve out a space where the chaos can't quell,
A haven of stillness, we know it so well.

With each quiet heartbeat, our spirits align,
In laughter and love, in the sweet intertwine.
The world may rush on, with its noise and demand,
But here in this moment, we firmly make stand.

So let us create, on this canvas of time,
A portrait of life, in rhythms and rhyme.
For in quiet together, our souls intertwine,
A masterpiece fashioned, forever divine.

9 781805 616399